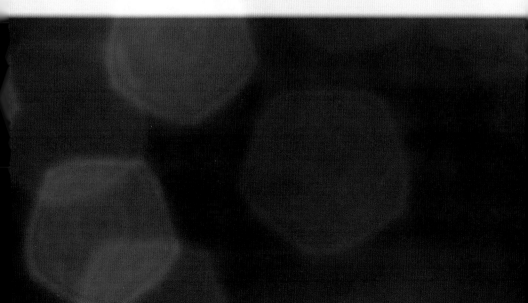

CONTEMPORARY LIVES

KANYE WEST

GRAMMY-WINNING HIP-HOP ARTIST & PRODUCER

ABDO
Publishing Company

KANYE WEST

GRAMMY-WINNING HIP-HOP ARTIST & PRODUCER

by Douglas Lynne

CREDITS

Published by ABDO Publishing Company, PO Box 398166,
Minneapolis, MN 55439. Copyright © 2013 by Abdo Consulting
Group, Inc. International copyrights reserved in all countries.
No part of this book may be reproduced in any form without
written permission from the publisher. The Essential Library™ is a
trademark and logo of ABDO Publishing Company.

Printed in the United States of America,
North Mankato, Minnesota
112012
012013

 THIS BOOK CONTAINS AT LEAST 10% RECYCLED MATERIALS.

Editor: Rebecca Felix
Series Designer: Emily Love

Cataloging-in-Publication Data
Lynne, Douglas.
 Kanye West: Grammy-winning hip-hop artist & producer / Douglas
Lynne.
   p. cm. -- (Contemporary lives)
Includes bibliographical references and index.
ISBN 978-1-61783-623-7
1. West, Kanye, 1977- --Juvenile literature. 2. Rap musicians--
United States--Biography--Juvenile literature. 1. Title.
782.421649092--dc15
[B]

2012945975

TABLE OF CONTENTS

A beaming Kanye West on the red carpet at the Grammy Awards in 2005

CHAPTER 1

Expecting to Win

||||||||||||||||||||||||||||||||||||||||||

n the heart of downtown Los
Angeles, California, the Staples
Center was packed with stars. It was
the night of February 13, 2005, and the
Grammy Awards were underway inside.
The time came for the Best Rap Album
nominees to be announced. Nominees
included albums by classic rap group the
Beastie Boys, rappers Jay-Z and Nelly,
and hip-hop singer and rapper LL Cool J.
Hip-hop singer, rapper, and producer

Kanye West's album *The College Dropout* rounded out the nominations. Acting as award announcer, actor Kevin Bacon held up the sealed envelope that contained the results. Relatively new rapper West felt sure he would win. The time had come to find out if he was right. Bacon opened the envelope and leaned toward the microphone. The award went to West for *The College Dropout*.

Dressed in all white with his signature attention to detail, a beaming West made his way to the stage to accept his award. The 28-year-old artist somehow looked both nervous and confident as he cautioned the audience that his acceptance speech was "gonna take a while."[1]

West's speech came in at under three minutes, but in that short time he displayed the many sides of his personality. He spoke humbly about his car accident a few years earlier. He thanked his fans, his mom, and everyone who had helped him. Then he switched to his characteristic cockiness, proclaiming he was going to celebrate hard. And finally, he poked a little fun at himself. A few months earlier, West had very publicly complained about losing the award for Best New Artist at a different music awards show. During the

West hoists his award for Best Rap Album in solemn victory at the end of his acceptance speech.

months leading up to the Grammys, that incident created media buzz and speculation, which West referenced during his acceptance speech. "Everybody wanted to know what I would do, if I didn't win," he said in a serious tone. Lifting his Grammy Award triumphantly, he ended his speech, "I guess we'll never know!"[2]

As of 2012, West had won a total of 18 Grammys, which was more than any artist in the previous ten years. Each of his five solo albums went platinum, which means each sold more than 1 million copies. West also sold 30 million digital downloads of his songs, making him one of the most downloaded musicians of all time.

West was nominated for a staggering ten awards that night—more than any other artist that year. Of those nominations, he earned two more awards later that evening: one for Best Rap Song for "Jesus Walks" and the other for cowriting Best R&B Song "You Don't Know My Name" by rhythm and blues (R&B) singer Alicia Keys.

||||||||||||||||||||||||||||||||||||||||||||||||||

CHART TOPPER, INDUSTRY CHANGER

Before taking the Grammys—and the hip-hop world—by storm, West spent years perfecting his technique. Initially known for his skills as a producer, he created beats for such performers as singer Keys, rappers Beanie Sigel and Ludacris, and, most notably, five of the 13 tracks on rapper Jay-Z's 2001 award-winning album *The Blueprint*.

Although he'd already found success for his production work, West truly wanted to be the guy on stage. He had a vision in his mind, and he was not going to give up. His mother, Donda West, remembered how, in the beginning, people frequently told her son no. No, he wasn't going to be signed to a label; no, he couldn't get up on stage. But being told no didn't stop West. He had a hustle mentality and a tenacity that could not be ignored, according to his mom. "Somebody had to reward that kind of persistence," she said.[3]

Following his Grammy Award wins in 2005, West's second album, *Late Registration,* topped the charts. It also won Best Rap Album at the Grammys in 2006. In 2007, West released the album *Graduation,* which went platinum. At the Grammys honoring music from that year, he won Best Rap Album, Best Rap Song, Best Rap Solo Performance, and Best Rap Performance Duo or Group. The streak of musical success continued in the following years.

But West hasn't limited himself just to making music. He has been keenly interested in fashion and has appeared regularly on the covers of magazines such as *Details* and *GQ.* He's held a front-row seat at major fashion shows for years, and he has also designed clothing. Additionally, before he discontinued it, he was "a first rate fashion editor for his blog," according to the *New York Times*. The newspaper noted in 2008 that, on his blog, West "often spotlights new brands . . . and products well before many of the top magazines."[4]

A multifaceted artist, West has often been outspoken about his talent. He has stormed the stage at more than one awards show, asserting his opinion when either he or someone he felt deserved to win lost out on an award. He has lashed out about things he thinks are wrong with society in the United States. Another thing West has been vocal about disliking is the way the press has portrayed him. For example, a 2007 article in *Harper's Bazaar* magazine described his lavish Los Angeles home and a large mural covering an entire ceiling that allegedly depicted West as an angel. West responded, "That made me so mad. Because who wants to hang out with a guy with an eight-foot picture of an angel of himself?"[5]

Despite his apparent triumphs, West seems perpetually disgruntled. His extreme successes and equally outrageous comments and behavior

His attitude and antics often lead to negative media buzz, but West's unique talent, style, and sound earn him much praise.

have garnered West his fair share of both praise and criticism. Many fans and media members have wondered whether he has a genuine gift or is simply brash and egotistical. Despite this speculation, it is undeniable that West has become a major and memorable force in hip-hop.

||||||||||

Kanye with his mother, Donda West

CHAPTER 2

Born Confident

|||||||||||||||||||||||||||||||||||||||||||||||||||||||||||||||||||||||||||||||||||||||||||

Kanye Omari West was born on June 8, 1977, in Douglasville, Georgia. Proud parents Ray West and Donda Williams had met just a few years before at Spelman College in Atlanta, Georgia. Ray was hired as a freelance photographer by Spelman College's public relations director. Donda worked in that same public relations department while studying for her master's degree at Atlanta University. The two began dating and married three months later on January 1, 1973, in Oklahoma City, Oklahoma, which was where Donda's parents lived. The newlyweds settled into married life in Atlanta. They lived in a town house Donda had bought shortly after starting work at Spelman. The two were intelligent, opinionated, and free-spirited. They also never intended to have kids. But that changed three years into their marriage when Donda said she was suddenly gripped by an overwhelming desire to have a child. As she later put it,

> I had made a decision with my head never to have children. But my body and my spirit had other plans. I think it was God selecting Ray and me right then to have the child who would become Kanye West.[1]

Donda later revealed in her memoir, *Raising Kanye: Life Lessons from the Mother of a Hip-Hop Superstar*, that although her husband was convinced he didn't want to be a dad, he considered the possibility to please her and then finally agreed. Donda recalled that during the time right after Kanye was born, Ray was a great husband and father. Shortly after Kanye was born,

Donda and Ray had not given much thought to names while Donda was pregnant with Kanye. But the couple did know they wanted their child to have a name that sounded strong and represented his African-American heritage. After giving birth, Donda and her mom began thumbing through a book of African names at the hospital. They found Kanye, which means "the only one" in Swahili, and Omari, which means "God the highest" in Swahili. Both Donda's mom and Ray also liked the idea that his initials would be K. O., which stands for "knockout" in boxing, when a boxer drops an opponent to the ground in victory. The name Kanye Omari became official.

Ray expanded his photography business. Ray began putting in more time building his business and less time with Donda and Kanye. In a heated argument, Donda confronted Ray, who confessed that work was his first priority. In that instant, Donda decided it was time to leave. She later said, "I certainly wasn't coming second to Ray's business. Not me and not Kanye."[2] Kanye was 11 months old when his parents separated. Ray and Donda's divorce became final when Kanye was three years old.

Kanye's father, Ray, was a member of the Black Panther Party, a photojournalist, and most recently, a spiritual counselor. His mother received a doctorate degree in English Education and became the chairwoman of the Chicago State University English Department, where she was a professor. These diverse and intellectual interests influenced Kanye from early on. In an interview with the newspaper magazine *USA Today*, Ray said of this influence on Kanye, "His mother and I never talked to him as if he was a kid. We always talked to him like he was an adult, and he sometimes had to catch up to the language. I'm a storyteller. I talk in analogies. . . . I've just sat back and been amazed at where he has taken it."[3]

In 1980, Donda finished her doctorate degree from Auburn University in Auburn, Alabama, which is a couple of hours from Atlanta. She began her teaching career at Morris Brown College in Atlanta. However, Donda was ready for a change of scenery. A main reason she had finally filed for divorce was because she wanted to leave Atlanta to start a new life. She just wasn't sure where she'd go. Then she met Larry Lewis from Chicago, Illinois, who was in Atlanta visiting a friend. Donda and Lewis began dating. Before long, Donda and Kanye moved to Chicago. Donda and Lewis's relationship lasted only a few months following her move.

In Chicago, Donda was offered and accepted a position as a professor of English at Chicago State University. Within a year, she bought a house on South Shore Drive, a distinguished area in Chicago. Donda and Kanye lived there for eight years in relative happiness and comfort. A man named Willie "Scotty" Scott dated Donda and lived with her and Kanye for a few of those years as well. Donda worked at the university from 1980 to 2004, mainly as a professor, but was also the chair of the English Department for six of those years.

Although Kanye was raised mainly by his mom, he had a connection to his dad. Donda later wrote that she never wanted to prevent them from being together. After moving to Chicago, Kanye spent summers with his father in Georgia. Kanye continued to stay in touch, but he has also called their relationship strained. Despite this, Ray has said, "There's never a phone call we don't end with 'I love you.'"[4]

Kanye spent much of his childhood in Chicago, Illinois.

SCHOOL AND SOCIAL SKILLS

At an early age, Kanye began showing advanced skills in certain areas. He made his own toys and began drawing when he was three. His mother remembers buying him a box of crayons that he used to draw things that kids twice his age couldn't. "He drew people—real people, not stick people. I was impressed by it."[5] She also recalls Kanye would draw common objects in unusual ways such as a purple banana or a blue orange. He knew bananas were yellow and oranges were orange, but if he wanted to color them differently, he did. His unique way of thinking became evident in other ways as well. Once his aunt took him to a lake where he saw ducks and claimed they were quacking the wrong way.

In Chicago, Kanye was initially enrolled in Professional Playhouse Preschool, but then transferred to a preschool at Chicago State University where his mom worked. He did well there, and by the time he was ready for kindergarten, his teachers claimed he was academically gifted. However, they also felt Kanye could use some help socially. Observations that

Kanye as a boy

he was slightly self-absorbed and didn't work
well with others were made, which are comments
still used to describe him today. However, Donda
decided the school was not a good fit, and Kanye
would not continue there. When Kanye was ready

for kindergarten, Donda searched for just the right place. She found it at the Vanderpoel Magnet School in Chicago.

In elementary school, when Kanye was approximately seven years old, he participated in several talent shows and contests. Kanye started rapping at approximately the same time, when he was in the third grade, but no one knew his secret desire of being a star would one day become reality. Kanye studied at Vanderpoel Magnet School until he was ten. Then he and Donda set off on an adventure abroad.

||||||||||||

魁星亭

Living in Nanjing, China, for one year as a child exposed Kanye to new ideas and experiences.

CHAPTER 3

Adventure and Music

|||||||||||||||||||||||||||||||||||||||||||||||||||||||||||

uring the 1987–1988 school year, when Kanye was ten, he and his mother spent one year in Nanjing, China, where Donda was a visiting English professor through a Fulbright Scholarship program between Nanjing University and Chicago State University. Kanye went to a Chinese elementary school in Nanjing where, although he was a fifth grader in the United States, he was put in a third-grade classroom because of the language barrier. Donda anticipated this would upset Kanye, but he quickly adapted. And although Kanye was one of the few foreign kids at his school, he quickly made friends. He also had a private tutor from Zimbabwe who tutored him in the broad topics similar to what was being taught to US fifth graders so Kanye wouldn't fall behind when he returned.

Kanye was generally easygoing and well behaved in China, but there were instances when his headstrong tendencies emerged. Donda recalled an incident between her son and his classroom teacher in China. In the winter, the classrooms in Kanye's school were quite cold and many students wore gloves. The gloves were required to be fingerless, but Kanye had a regular pair with covered fingers. When his teacher attempted to take Kanye's gloves, he kicked her, and Donda was called to the school. Through an interpreter, Donda apologized and asked her son to do the same. Kanye did apologize, but with his eyes averted. Donda scolded him, "Kanye, you know you're to look at people when you're speaking to them. Eye contact is important. Why in the world would you look down at the floor?" However, it seems Kanye had absorbed a part of the culture Donda was not aware of. As Donda recalled, "He then explained to me that to look at the teacher would be rude and disrespectful. I had never realized that until that day."[1]

After a time, Donda took Kanye out of school in China to homeschool him because he wasn't excelling. To gain cultural exposure outside the classroom, Donda also made sure she and her son took every advantage of their year abroad. They

CHINA MEMORIES

Kanye learned to speak some Chinese while in China, but Donda believed Kanye had forgotten all but a few words of the language by the time he reached adulthood. Despite forgetting the language, though, Donda said their time in China remained one of the most memorable years of their lives. In addition to the many cultural experiences the two absorbed, Donda was surprised to discover a certain way Kanye imparted some American culture on his Chinese peers. One day, Donda met Kanye as he was devouring a skewer of lamb's meat, a snack sold on street corners and in parks in China. She knew she hadn't given him much pocket money and wondered how he could have bought the snack. It turned out that Kanye, who knew how to break-dance but had been forbidden by Donda to do so for fear he would break his neck, was charging Chinese children to watch him dance. Although Donda was slightly amused at his moneymaking venture, she was also a little upset.

Donda and Kanye experienced Chinese culture during their year abroad by visiting historic Chinese sites such as the Great Wall of China.

visited the historic site of the Great Wall of China and the ancient mountain range Huangshuan, or Yellow Mountain. They took a boat from the city of Canton to Hong Kong, an island region that is a territory of China. They also visited the Southeast Asian country of Thailand. In addition to these cultural excursions, Kanye also had the opportunity in China to participate in many extracurricular activities. He took lessons in Tai Chi, an ancient Chinese art of meditation and exercise, and he had private art lessons twice a week in addition to his studies with his tutor to keep up his US education.

When their year in China was up, Donda and Kanye returned to Chicago. Kanye reenrolled in Vanderpoel for sixth grade in 1988. In middle school, he began to focus on his passions. He decided he wanted to design video games. "I wanted to do everything: I wanted to design the characters, design the backgrounds. I would be studying different things and try to come up with a new idea," Kanye said.[2] His mom bought him the necessary design programs, and Kanye remembers especially liking the one managing sound. After that, Donda said she never had to worry where Kanye was, "because he was sitting right there in front of that keyboard."[3]

Kanye found others who shared his interest. When he was approximately 12 or 13 years old, he and a small group of friends practiced music at the Wests' home. Kanye wrote "Green Eggs and Ham," the first rap song his mother remembers him writing, and he wanted to record it. Most studios charged more money than Donda was willing to pay to record the song. But Kanye didn't give up. He found out about a studio that charged just $25 an hour, a sum Donda was willing to pay. The studio was in the basement of a house and was less than professional—the microphone was hanging from a wire clothes hanger. But Kanye was excited, so Donda paid the $25, and Kanye got his recording.

Once Kanye finished eighth grade at Vanderpoel Magnet School, Donda went on a quest to find the best high school for her son. She found it in the Polaris School for Individual Education in Cook County, Illinois. By this time, Kanye was consumed with music. He knew he was going to be a star, and he was focused on that goal. "I thought I was going to get signed back when I was 13 years old," he said.[4]

At 14, Kanye got his first sampling keyboard. He had saved almost $500, and for Christmas in 1991, his mother gave him $1,000. It was just enough to buy the keyboard. With the instrument, Kanye created his first beat. By this time, Kanye had decided he wanted to be a rapper. "And in the seventh grade, I figured if I wanted to be a rapper, I had to have something to rap over," he said. "So I started doing beats. And I really got serious around

After completing his studies at Vanderpoel, Kanye enrolled at the Polaris School for Individual Education in ninth grade.

age 14, when I even charged people like, $50 for a beat here and there."[5]

Donda recalled that Kanye was always working odd jobs to save enough money to build his bedroom studio. Soon, he was able to get turntables, a mixer, and a drum machine. Kanye would spend hours mixing, rapping, and writing. His social life became centered around his music studio in his room as well. Donda welcomed her son's friends and their music into their home. "At times it was nerve-wracking with all the noise. But I preferred a little discomfort to him being in the streets."[6]

Kanye started his own production company, Kon-Man Productions, and named his friend Mikkey Halsted, a Chicago-based emcee, vice president of the company. Halsted said,

> *"There was a whole circle of us back then, such as Kanye, Rhymefest, GLC, and me. We would all work on songs together, come up with patterns or lines, and help each other over all. Sometimes we'll call each other on the phone and we'll tell each other which lines we like, or if the chorus should be reworked, things like that."[7]*

When Kanye was approximately 14, he met one of his mentors, a beatsmith and producer named No I.D. No I.D.'s mother went to school at Chicago State University, where Donda taught

CREATING A BEAT

To create a beat is to build the foundation of sound for music. It is the basic rhythm that is created as a base for other sounds, such as recorded vocals or instruments, to be layered on top. A beat is typically created electronically, using sounds from a computer music program and an electronic keyboard, which are then recorded when the desired sound is achieved.

Even after Kanye became a star, he and hometown mentor and producer No I.D. remained friends. "We never really changed our relationship," said No I.D. in a 2007 interview with *Entertainment Weekly*. "When we talk, we talk like we've been talking every single day. A lot of our conversation has been either life issues or music. He's younger than me, so it was never like he was my peer. Maybe he was 14 and I was 20, so he was the kid to me. I helped him out. And now he's not the kid, but it still kind of feels like it when we talk. But I definitely respect everything he's accomplished. I'm proud of him."[8]

English. The two mothers met, and Donda asked No I.D.'s mother to talk to her son about teaching Kanye everything he knew about music. Then approximately 20 years old, No I.D. was working with future rap star Common, who was then called Common Sense. No I.D. had a basement studio at his house where Kanye would become a frequent visitor. At first, No I.D. just gave Kanye things to work on to keep him busy, but he soon discovered that Kanye was talented and began encouraging and nurturing him. In No I.D.'s studio, Kanye absorbed techniques and tutorials from the producer as he worked. Between these experiences and his constant electronic tinkering, rapping, and making beats in his bedroom, Kanye's skills as a producer grew.

Kanye was also improving his skills as a rapper and wasn't afraid to challenge others, sparring back and forth with lyrics created on the spot. "He was this young hungry like confident cat that would come around and he would always want to battle with me on the mic," Common said.[9] Common wouldn't be the last person Kanye challenged in the music world.

MUSIC OVER SCHOOL

From the time he entered school until he was 14 and in ninth grade, Kanye was on the honor role at school. In the 1991–1992 school year, however, his grades began declining as he focused on his music. Because she knew he was more than capable of doing well, Donda felt there was no excuse for him to do poorly and encouraged him to try to do better. But she didn't punish him when his grades slipped. She understood his music was more important to him than his schoolwork.

Kanye working on art in a high school class

By the time he was in eleventh grade, Kanye's grades continued sliding, and by his final year in high school his mom had to urge him to graduate. He did graduate from the Polaris School in the spring of 1995, and then, surprisingly, took a path that seemed unlikely: college.

||||||||||

West's high school senior portrait

CHAPTER 4

Musical
Ambitions

||||||||||||||||||||||||||||||||||||||||||||||||||||||||||||||||

lthough his behavior in high school suggested education was perhaps not very important to West, he went to college after graduating high school. He first went to the American Academy of Art in downtown Chicago, where he could follow his interests in design. But West eventually decided he didn't want to pursue a career in art and dropped out.

At his mother's prodding, West then enrolled at Chicago State University, where Donda taught English. Following in his mother's footsteps, West became an English major because he liked words. He also liked the idea that because his mother was chair of the English Department, he wouldn't have to stand in long lines to register for classes. Donda picked his classes, filled out his registration form, and signed it. In college, West learned more about the basics of language and good writing—information he could apply when writing lyrics for his music. Like many rappers, West wrote about what he knew and experienced. Although many rappers' music focuses on the gangster lifestyle, it was foreign to West. He grew up in a middle-class home, was well educated, and was attracted to preppy fashions—sport coats, polo shirts, and sunglasses.

West's first semester at Chicago State University went well, but during the second semester he ran into trouble. Because Donda was faculty, she was able to speak with colleagues and find out how her son was doing. In addition to hearing he was smart and a good writer, she was told her son often skipped class and didn't always turn in his work. West spent more time in the college's music department and the student union than in his classes.

> "With school, I just didn't really want to be there. I was like, 'How do these credits apply to what I want to do in my life?' So I would take courses that I could use a little bit: piano, speech, public speaking, English—which all helps me now."[2]
>
> —*WEST ON BEING IN COLLEGE*

Throughout this time, West pushed to make himself known in the hip-hop community. "He was always at some venue in Chicago trying to be seen and heard, trying to break into the hip-hop game," Donda recalled.[1] West never stopped making music, and his persistence paid off. In 1996, just after his nineteenth birthday, West had a meeting in New York with Sony. West had made a beat on a song No I.D. produced for Atlanta rapper Jermaine Dupri. This made the aspiring producer and rapper visible to Sony, which was Dupri's record label. The company flew West to New York City, picked him up in a limo from the airport, and whisked him to their offices on Madison Avenue.

He met with several executives: Donnie Ienner, then-chairman of Sony Music Group, and Michael Mauldin, who at that time was the president and head of Sony's black music division. The executives grilled West. They wanted to know how he was different from other rappers. They weren't going to be interested in him if he was just the same as everyone else. The characteristically quick-witted West was not prepared to answer, however. He had assumed being talented was enough to impress the executives. However, he did brag that he was going to become a bigger star than Dupri, who was quite popular at the time. West didn't know that Mauldin was Dupri's father. He did not get the deal.

Upon returning to Chicago, West redoubled his efforts to make music. He worked even harder producing music and writing raps. In 1996, he became part of a music group called the Go Getters. The group included other Chicago rappers GLC, Timmy G, Really Doe, and Arrowstar. The Go Getters produced a handful of songs and did some radio appearances and publicity shots. Some of these songs made it onto a collection of tracks titled *World Record Holders,* which was produced by Kon-Man Productions and included the works of several

Jermaine Dupri found success in the rap industry as a rapper and producer.

artists. It was distributed throughout the Chicago area in 1999 but never released as an official album.

West spent another semester and a half at Chicago State University before dropping out in 1998. Donda was at first upset and surprised, but she accepted his decision. She made a deal with him. He could continue to live at home for one more year as he tried to make it as a musician. As part of the deal, West would have to pay $200 a month for rent. To make money while trying to launch his music career, West got a job working as a busboy in a local restaurant. But he quit before he even started, deciding that kind of work wasn't what he wanted. He then landed a series of telemarketing jobs and did fairly well at that type of work.

With work to pay his rent secured, West began spending an increasing amount of time on

PROMOTING SCHOOL

Although West dropped out of college, he takes time to let students know education is important. In December 2005, West appeared at a high school in Santa Monica, California, for a concert and tuition giveaway. His charity, the Kanye West Foundation, teamed with Musicland for the Free U. College Giveaway, where students could register at Musicland stores to win a $150,000 college scholarship. At the event, West said, "It is true you can be successful without [college], but this is a hard world, a real world, and you want every advantage you can have. . . . Life is hard. Take advantage of your opportunities."[3]

West also appeared in Chicago on June 8, 2010, his thirty-third birthday, for his third annual Stay in School concert. Held at Farragut Career Academy, the concert included other rappers. The artists also visited two other Chicago public schools—Marshall and Julian—to reward the kids for improving their grades, attendance, and behavior.

music, whenever he could fit it in around work. "Whenever I would finish work, I would be up until 4:00 in the morning . . . focusing on my dream and praying for the day where I could just do that all the time," he said.[4] Donda became less welcoming of the constant sounds that rocked the walls of the house. Additionally, more and more people began coming to the house, where they would have to pass by Donda's room to get to West's bedroom studio. He had been selling beats to local producers for $200 to $500, which kept his dream of making it in the music industry alive.

Then West got a big break. He had started working with Gravity, a Chicago rapper who had landed a record deal. Donda recalled that Gravity bought beats created by her son for $8,000, a large sum of money for West at the time. It was at this point that Donda realized West was on his way to making a successful career in music. He had devoted less than a year to hip-hop, and through selling beats he had saved up enough money to move out.

Donda helped West find an apartment in the Beverly district on the southwest side of Chicago. It had a small room West could use as a studio. At first the landlord was reluctant to rent to

West, thinking he was too young to handle the responsibility. But Donda assured him her son was responsible and if he had any problems, she'd be on hand to back up West. However, it turned out the landlord didn't like the many visitors Kanye had coming over because of his music, and he wanted West to leave. West became convinced that if he wanted to make it big in the hip-hop world, he'd have to go somewhere new. He wasn't quite sure where he wanted to go—maybe Atlanta, maybe New York City. West and his mother agreed that if he wanted to work in New York, he should live in nearby New Jersey—a safer and less expensive option than New York itself. West moved to Newark, New Jersey, in an apartment that was across from Penn Station. At Penn Station, West could catch a train to New York whenever he needed to. West's group, the Go Getters, split up when he headed east.

In New York, West began trying to sell his demos around the island of Manhattan. One of these demos made its way to Kyambo "Hip-Hop" Joshua, the artists and repertoire (A&R) director at Roc-A-Fella Records, a hip-hop record label started in 1995 by rapper Jay-Z and two partners.

In the music industry, A&R is shorthand for Artists & Repertoire. This is a department at a record label, and the shorthand for the people that work within it. A record label A&R rep helps the label search for new, talented artists and get them signed. Once the artist has signed with the label, the A&R person oversees contract negotiations and the recording process, acting as the communicator between the artist and the label. The A&R person helps pull together the right songs, collaborating with professionals such as producers and songwriters, and finds a studio. The A&R person also monitors trends in the music industry to make sure albums created are hip, relevant, and will be a hit. A&R reps help facilitate the marketing of the album release and any promotional performances.

Impressed with what he heard, Joshua decided to put West in a studio session with Jay-Z. Damon Dash, cofounder of Roc-A-Fella, also felt West had talent.

Well established in the world of rap by 2001, Jay-Z put out his sixth album, *The Blueprint,* that year. It was heralded as one of his most expressive and soulful albums. The success and praise of Jay-Z's album was also a big break for West, who produced many of the tracks on the album. From

Jay-Z and Damon Dash in 2002

working on *The Blueprint* together, however, West's relationship with Jay-Z, and Dash's relationship with both men, became complicated.

With Roc-A-Fella, West was helping produce hit after hit for hip-hop singer Keys and rappers Ludacris, Common, and Cam'ron. But when West asked to make his own records, Jay-Z and Dash weren't convinced West could do it with his preppy image and lack of street credibility. At the time,

East Coast rap music lagged behind the fresh funk sounds of West Coast rappers such as Dr. Dre, Tupac Shakur, and Snoop Dogg. Because of this difference, Dash felt introducing West, who had an image very different from what was average and accepted within that genre, was risky.

In 2002, West almost signed with Capitol Records as a rapper. Joe "3H" Weinberger, a hip-hop producer and A&R executive for Capitol Records, thought West had talent as a producer and saw his potential to make it as a rapper. West was just about to sign the dotted line of the contract when, at the last minute, someone in the company told the president they thought West was a nobody producer/rapper who wouldn't sell well. West did not get the deal. He was disappointed, but he didn't give up.

Aware of the near-deal with Capitol Records, Roc-A-Fella at last decided to sign West to their label as a rapper, although executives were still unsure of his ability as a rapper. As Jay-Z put it, "We figured if we kept him close, at the very least we'd still have some hot beats."[5] West was about to prove himself as a talented rapper not only to the skeptics at Roc-A-Fella, but to the world.

||||||||||

The rise of West's career coincided with his healing from a serious car crash.

CHAPTER 5

Crash and Success

||||||||||||||||||||||||||||||||||||||||||||||||

n 2002, West kept busy working in the studio. Well known by then for his skills as a producer, he was working in Los Angeles on his rapping debut that autumn when an event occurred that affected his future career and put his life in danger. West worked in a Los Angeles sound studio until the early hours of the morning on October 23. Leaving the studio, he got in his car and headed toward his hotel.

En route at the intersection of Santa Monica and Wiltshire Boulevards, West was jolted forward, and his face slammed against the steering wheel of the car. It was later determined that the accident, in which West crashed into another car, occurred because he had fallen asleep at the wheel.

Upon impact, the airbag of West's Lexus deployed. He was pinned down and in horrible pain. West heard ambulance sirens approach. Paramedics and firemen arrived on the scene with the Jaws of Life, a tool used to tear into vehicles and pry out trapped accident victims. West's memory became foggy, and he may have passed out. The next thing he remembers was being on his way to Cedars-Sinai Hospital in Los Angeles.

Amid the confusion, West managed to contact his girlfriend Sumeke Rainey on his cell phone and told her to call his mom. Rainey called Donda immediately. After receiving the news from Rainey, Donda tried calling her son. West answered, and they had a short exchange in which he apologized to her for hurting himself before being cut off by a rescue worker. Donda and Rainey were on the next plane out of Chicago to Los Angeles.

In January 2012, rapper DJ Whoo Kid claimed he was with West just minutes before West's 2002 car accident. He also claimed being tired wasn't the only factor leading to the crash. Kid claimed West was upset because things hadn't gone well for him in the studio. "It was me, Beanie Siegel, Kanye and 3H. We were all in the studio and [rapper] Luda[cris] was in town," said Kid.[1] West wanted to impress Ludacris, but it was early in his career, and he lacked the experience to get everything right. According to Kid, West left the studio upset and minutes later had the accident. Since the story was revealed, however, there has been speculation whether the details are accurate.

Once at the hospital, West's mother reported that he was dropped on the ground of the emergency room, which he said hurt even more than the accident itself. She also said her son waited in the emergency room for hours before being treated. After that, West underwent additional hours of tests at the hospital to determine the damage caused from the accident. His head had swelled to several times its normal size, he had nasal fractures that wouldn't stop bleeding, and his jaw was broken in three places. Decisions had to be made about whether reconstructive surgery was possible. Donda met

MEDIA BUZZ SURROUNDING THE ACCIDENT

with an excellent surgeon who assured her he could restore West's face.

The day of the surgery, Donda, Rainey, and some of West's family from the Los Angeles area gathered at the hospital. The surgeon informed them the procedure would take approximately two and a half hours. The family sat in a waiting room, joined hands, and prayed. After four hours, the doctor emerged from the operating room. Things had taken longer because the surgical team had needed to take some additional X-rays. The hospital staff reported to West's family that he might require further surgery. West's face was still very swollen, and his jaw was wired shut to give his jaw fractures time to heal. West was in a lot of pain. He would have to stay in the hospital for a total of two weeks, but his mother stayed by his side.

When West was released from the hospital, his jaw was still wired shut. Donda helped her son pack his things, and they moved to the W Hotel in Los Angeles. Donda made sure West took his medicine and tried to find things he could eat. Because his jaw was wired shut, West could only eat what he could get through a straw. Donda fed him smoothies, soup, and juice.

As he healed, West lost no time getting back to work. According to his mom, he'd never actually stopped working. From his hospital bed, he thought of lyrics to describe his ordeal and began rapping them through his wired jaws. West convinced Roc-A-Fella he was up to returning to the studio to produce some more beats for other rappers. Then, three weeks after being released from the hospital, his jaw still wired shut, West recorded a song. The song was based off the lyrics he thought up while in the hospital. The resulting song, "Through the Wire," convinced Roc-A-Fella he was ready to create his own album. West's jaw was wired for approximately two months.

According to West, the hospital staff had wired his jaw incorrectly, and he had to have it rebroken and set correctly.

While West worked on his first album in 2003, "Through the Wire" was released on September 30 as a single. It spent 21 weeks on the *Billboard* Hot 100 list and peaked at Number 15. The song is backed with vocal samples from pop idol Chaka Khan's song "Through the Fire." West had finally made a name for himself as a rapper.

West also wanted to be known for giving back to others. In 2003, he announced the formation of the Kanye West Foundation. The foundation's goal was to help combat high school dropout rates. It closed in 2011.

While working on his album, West also continued producing beats for other artists. In 2003 alone, songs with beats he created, including rapper Ludacris's song "Stand Up," Jay-Z's "'03 Bonnie & Clyde," and Keys's hit "You Don't Know My Name" debuted. In addition to producing, West also had the chance to do some rap collaborations that year. On "Slow Jamz," he raps with fellow artist Twista and actor and

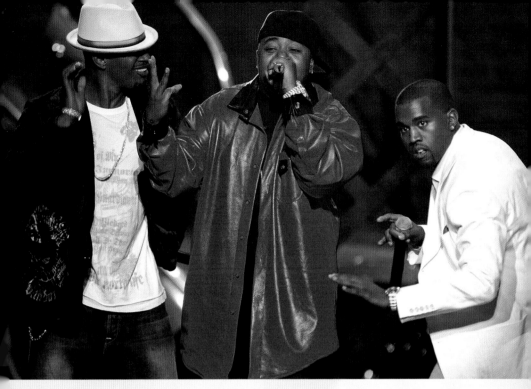

From left, Jamie Foxx, Twista, and West's song "Slow Jamz" was all three artists' first song to hit Number 1.

rapper Jamie Foxx. The song hit Number 1 on the *Billboard* Hot 100 list in February 2004. "Slow Jamz" was also nominated for a Best Rap/Sung Collaboration Grammy Award in 2005.

THE COLLEGE DROPOUT

West's first album, *The College Dropout*, was released on February 10, 2004. It sold more than 440,000 copies in its first week of release.

In addition to "Through the Wire," West raps about many personal experiences and emotions. Many songs also raise questions or comment on social issues, including race, religion, and education. The intro to the album kicks off with a teacher asking West to deliver his high school graduation speech. On the next track, "We Don't Care," West raps a line speaking to the low educational and career expectations society often applies to young black teens: "We wasn't supposed to make it past 25/ Joke's on you, we still alive."[3]

On "All Falls Down," which became his first Top 10 hit, West criticizes "consumerism as an expression of self-hatred rooted in history," as one reviewer explained it.[4] Another hit, "Jesus Walks,"

DONDA UPS SALES

When *The College Dropout* released, West's mom went out and bought ten copies at a Best Buy store. The employee was completing the purchase transaction and made a remark about the number of copies Donda had bought. Donda confessed she was the artist's mother. However, the clerk didn't believe her, arguing that West's mom wouldn't have to buy his CD; her son would likely give her copies for free. Donda later said, "I didn't have to buy it, I wanted to buy it. In fact, I came back a couple of days later and bought more. I wanted his first CD to hit the charts."[5]

finds West rapping about religion, an uncommon rap topic at the time. The song gained a following for promoting a positive message, which West embraced, even hoping that other rappers would follow his lead.

The album was praised as inventive and adventurous and a departure from what was standard rap at the time. Amid his musical debut, West also introduced the world to his egotistical side. He said of his debut:

> *I know what I'm doing. I might have designed the sound of music for the next decade. If you ask me about my music, about how I've impacted the world, I will argue that my first album is one of the best freshman albums ever. That's not me being a fan of me, but me being a fan of music.*[6]

G.O.O.D MUSIC

Extending the positive vibe in his life at the time, West started Getting Out Our Dreams (G.O.O.D.) Music. G.O.O.D. Music is not a label, but rather it does production work and then works in conjunction with other labels for distribution.

As GLC once described it, "it's basically a family and like a production company . . . you get a distribution deal and if you're a G.O.O.D Music artist, then you come out on G.O.O.D Music and the distribution deal."[7] In 2011, G.O.O.D. Music and record label Island Def Jam Music Group signed a long-term agreement that made G.O.O.D. Music into a more formal record label.

Nearing the end of 2004, West had already enjoyed quite a successful year. Then, in November, he was nominated for three American Music Awards: Favorite Male Artist, Favorite Album (*The College Dropout*), and Best New Artist. West did not win any awards at that year's American Music Awards. It seemed losing Best New Artist hit him hardest—and he did not react well. Country singer Gretchen Wilson won the award, and West complained backstage that he was the rightful winner and had been robbed of the award. He also made claims that he might boycott that particular awards show in the future. The comments were publicized, and a month later West apologized to Wilson. He also apologized to his "black role models, like Jay-Z and Oprah Winfrey, for being overemotional. I was doing a disservice

West onstage with country singer Gretchen Wilson as she accepted the American Music Award for Best New Artist in 2004

to everything my forefathers have done to allow black people to get to this place."[8] The entire incident created negative media buzz, which is never welcome for a newer artist. And it would not be the last of such occurrences. West was starting a pattern: blurting out whatever came to his mind and acting irrationally just to apologize for it later.

ROC-A-FELLA TRANSITION

In December 2004, a much-publicized falling out between Jay-Z and Dash culminated in their sale of Roc-A-Fella. Speculation that there were tensions between the two began as far back as 2002, when Dash began signing rappers to the Roc-A-Fella label without consulting anyone. By December 2004, Def Jam Recordings, a major label of Island Def Jam Music Group, approached Jay-Z about a buyout. Roc-A-Fella had sold Def Jam a 50 percent stake in the company in 1997 for $1.5 million. Jay-Z went to Dash and told Dash he could sell his share of Roc-A-Fella to Def Jam, where Jay-Z had also been offered the role of president, and then give up some master recordings to one of Jay-Z's albums in order to keep the Roc-A-Fella name. Dash wanted to keep the name but refused the offer. Jay-Z left Roc-A-Fella and became the CEO and president of Def Jam. The label bought the remaining 50 percent of Roc-A-Fella for $10 million—and kept the name Roc-A-Fella as a label under parent company Def Jam.

Jay-Z and Def Jam also took most of the Roc-A-Fella artists, including West. Since then, West has made it no secret that although Dash was

Jay-Z, Damon Dash, and Russell Simmons, one of the founders of Def Jam, in 2003

instrumental in getting him started, he considers Jay-Z his true mentor. West later admitted that his following Jay-Z to Def Jam was disloyal. During a 2005 interview with MTV, host Sway prodded West, "So Dame Dash pretty much put his stamp on you and validated you . . . [but] you chose to stick with Jay-Z. . . . Do you think that's disloyal?" West answered, "Um, yeah." He then continued:

But you gotta make that decision. I felt like with the relationship that me and Jay built after I was on Roc-A-Fella, we had built a different type of relationship, it was a working musical relationship because of the production, and I built more like a business relationship with Dame. . . . And not to be cliché, but it's like I was between a rock and a hard place. And it was just like if your parents were to divorce.[9]

West has since stated that he is very close with Jay-Z and that he admires him greatly. He also aspires to reach the level of his rap idol through competition. "I idolize him for certain aspects

"BIG BROTHER" JAY-Z

In his 2007 song "Big Brother," West raps about the ups and downs of working with Jay-Z. In parts sentimental and in parts brutally honest, the song has been credited as a brilliant example of how West will take on a topic most other rappers won't touch and make it work. For his part, Jay-Z has said it's one of his favorites.

"I think it's a fair portrayal from a little brother's perspective. . . . At Roc-A-Fella, we've always lived by tough love. Everyone knows that. It's nothing given. Everyone has to work for theirs, and that's how you make strong individuals, by not carrying them. That's how you make a Kanye West. You make him fight for his position."[10]

West and Jay-Z developed a close working relationship at Roc-A-Fella.

and he would be my greatest competition, so if I'm writing a rap, I'm writing a rap to beat Jay," he said.[11] The relationship would continue to influence West's career, and the two rappers would go on to make a lot of music together.

||||||||||

In 2005, West's success and fame rose. His first album was nominated and won awards, and his second was met with praise.

CHAPTER 6

Changing Hip-Hop

||||||||||||||||||||||||||||||||||||||||||||||||||

y 2005, *The College Dropout* was a success, the Roc-A-Fella label and most of its artists were settled in at Def Jam, and West was keeping busy. In April of that year, West made *Time* magazine's list of the year's 100 most influential people in the world. Many facets of West's personality influenced his career. In addition to unique lyrics and beats, he also brought a new look and style

to hip-hop. His preppy look that had sometimes made him seem less credible to members of the rap industry was no longer a problem. In fact, his fitted clothing distinguished West from the rest of hip-hop artists, who most often wore oversized T-shirts and baggy jeans.

West was also distinguishing himself as something of a loose cannon. On August 18, West appeared on an MTV program called *All Eyes On Kanye West*. During an interview with host Sway, he discussed his childhood and his parents, his career, and the world of rap. He also made several controversial comments about homosexuality. West stated that traditional rap culture is homophobic. West, however, felt he was different. He wanted to distinguish himself as a rapper who went on the record claiming this wasn't right. His

ALBUM THEMES ||||||||||||||||||||||||||||||||||||||||||||||||||||||||||||||||||||||||||||||||||||||||||||

Though Kanye never finished college, the influence of his mother's strong support of education can be seen in the college-themed names of his first three albums— *The College Dropout*, *Late Registration*, and *Graduation*. Many of West's album covers also include a teddy bear. West has said he likes stuffed animals in general and that people give him teddy bears often.

West signed copies of his album *Late Registration* at an exclusive appearance at Tower Records in New York City.

pronouncement about homophobia in the rap industry made a lot of waves in the media.

Nearly two weeks later, West released his second album, *Late Registration*, on August 30. The album took approximately one year to create. West felt the album had to walk a fine line between sounding like his first and being something fresh and new. "I didn't want to play it boring and safe," he said. "I also didn't want to innovate too much. Second albums, man, they're even scarier than first ones."[1] The album included five singles, including "Heard 'Em Say," "Touch the Sky," and the most popular song, "Gold Digger," a catchy hit that was a collaboration with Foxx. The song shot to Number 1 on the *Billboard* Hot 100 chart and stayed there for ten weeks.

The album also contains a touching ode to West's mother, "Hey Mama." In the song, he raps: "(Hey Mama), I know I act a fool, but I promise you I'm goin' back to school/I appreciate what you allowed for me/And I just want you to be proud of me."[2] He worked on it for months to get it just right, "to make it as great as she is."[3] Most critics applauded *Late Registration*, and *Rolling Stone* called the album "an undeniable triumph."[4] *Late Registration* and its songs were nominated for a total of seven Grammy Awards in 2006. West won three: Best Rap Song ("Diamonds from Sierra Leone"), Best Rap Solo Performance ("Gold Digger"), and Best Rap Album.

Many of the victims of Hurricane Katrina were evacuated to Houston, Texas. West and his parents went to Houston to see how they could help. On the first day of their stay, the Wests visited the Astrodome, where thousands of people were being sheltered. That same day, the Wests visited two area churches where more hurricane victims were living. West talked with the people and asked what they needed. The Kanye West Foundation then donated to the Hurricane Katrina relief, and West contributed to a CD that was made to benefit victims of the disaster.

CREATING MORE CONTROVERSY

Just three days after *Late Registration* was released, West appeared on television for a live benefit concert. The benefit was for victims of Hurricane Katrina, a devastating natural disaster that wreaked havoc on the southeast coast of the United States in late August 2005. The city of New Orleans, Louisiana, had been hit especially hard. West and actor and comedian Mike Myers were supposed to deliver scripted lines on the show to incite public support for relief efforts. But West strayed from his scripted lines. The government had received scrutiny and criticism for appearing to neglect particular areas hit by the hurricane. Crime rates shot up in some of the poorer neighborhoods, and many felt government officials were doing nothing about it. West felt the oversight had to do with race. "I hate the way they portray [black people] in the media. You see a black family, [the screen] says, 'They're looting.' You see a white family, it says, 'They're looking for food.'"[5] Cohost Myers looked stunned and uncomfortable by his comments and tried to get back on track with the script. But West then concluded by accusing then-president George W. Bush of being prejudiced, saying, "George Bush doesn't care about black people."[6]

A media frenzy followed, with both critics and supporters of West's remarks. Some media members and celebrities praised West for his outspokenness. When NBC decided to censor West's remarks for a later viewing of the benefit, Reverend Al Sharpton said, "I think they should let Kanye say what needs to be said and let the president defend it if he wants to."[7] Jay-Z said "I'm backing Kanye 100 percent. This is America. You should be able to say what you want to say. We have freedom of speech."[8]

Mike Myers, *left*, and West, *right*, appeared on comedy sketch show *Saturday Night Live* approximately one month after West's Hurricane Katrina fund-raiser outburst to make light of the incident.

But others were taken aback by West's comments. The producer of the program said he would not edit the program to eliminate political statements, and that he thought "people understand that politicizing this will certainly not be a smart thing to do as far as inspiring people to call in and rally around this cause."[9] Discussion over West's outburst would continue however, even long after it happened. Even President Bush himself recalled in his memoir five years later that West's remark was the lowest point in his presidency.

||||||||||

West and Alexis Phifer in 2007

CHAPTER 7

Love and Loss

|||||||||||||||||||||||||||||||||||||||||||||||||||||||||||||||||||||||||||||||||||||||||||||

West's confident attitude did more than boost his music career and create media buzz. The combination of confidence and good looks also made him popular with women. From the time he became a public figure, West has seemed never to be without an attractive woman nearby. One such woman was fashion designer Alexis Phifer, whom he dated off and on from 2002 to 2006. In August 2006, he proposed to her. In light of their track record for breaking up, some media sources claimed West's decision to tie the knot with Phifer was made simply because he wanted to honor his mother's wishes to make the relationship official. She said yes, and the two were engaged until 2008, but they would never marry.

Three months later, West was again in the news for something less positive. The MTV European Music Awards ceremony took place in Copenhagen, Denmark, on November 2, 2006. West was nominated in three categories at the night's awards. Though he was named Best Hip-Hop Artist, West crashed the stage when his video "Touch the Sky" lost the award for Best Video to Justice vs. Simian's "We Are Your Friends." Though he had been known to complain when he didn't win honors he thought he deserved, rushing the stage was a shocking new development. Once onstage, West claimed he should win because his video "cost a million dollars, Pamela Anderson was in it. I was jumping across canyons. . . . If I don't win, the awards show loses credibility."[1] It was the first time West actually stormed a stage, interrupting other performers. Unfortunately, it would not be the last.

Evel Knievel preparing to take off in his rocket during his famous stunt attempt at the Snake River Canyon in 1974

"TOUCH THE SKY" TROUBLE

While all this was happening, the actual video West defended in his stage rush was coming under legal fire. The "Touch the Sky" video reenacted an actual trick iconic stuntman Evel Knievel had performed in 1974 at the Snake River Canyon in Idaho. In the original stunt, Knievel was launched from a rocket and was supposed to touch the sky. However, his parachute deployed midair, ruining the stunt. West's video has many similarities: he plays a character he calls "Evel Kanyevel," and when a rocket launches, his character flies through the air for a brief moment and then crashes in flames.

The rocket looks exactly like the one Knievel used in his original stunt, and the jumpsuit West is wearing is similar to the one Knievel wore.

Knievel found the entire video distasteful and sued West for using his likeness. In December, he stated he was suing West and Roc-A-Fella for damaging his reputation. "That video that Kanye West put out is the most worthless piece of crap I've ever seen in my life, and he uses my image to catapult himself on the public," he said.[2] The lawsuit would drag well into 2007.

RAP RIVALRY

After approximately two years of work, by September 2007 West was ready to release his third album, *Graduation*. West started working on *Graduation* right after the release of his second album, *Late Registration*, and he recorded it in New York City and Los Angeles. West's third album was a success, with hits such as "Can't Tell Me Nothing," "Stronger," and "Good Life."

Graduation was released on September 11, 2007, the same day 50 Cent, another popular

West and 50 Cent faced each other at the MTV Video Music Awards in 2007, days before their competing albums were released.

rapper, came out with his album *Curtis*. According to West, he chose the competitive date on purpose to incite publicity.

Antonio "L.A." Reid, then-chairman of Island Def Jam Music Group, claimed the release date for West's album was actually timed to coincide with the MTV Video Music Awards that year. Just two days before its debut, the 2007 MTV Video Music Awards were held in Las Vegas, Nevada. West was up for five nominations: Male Artist of the Year, Quadruple Threat of the Year, Video of the Year, Best Direction, and Best Editing for "Stronger." West won none of them. Though he didn't storm the stage, he did once again complain to the press about his losses. He felt he should have opened the show on the main stage with his hit song "Stronger" and felt betrayed that he hadn't.

Leading up to their coinciding releases, West and 50 Cent traded trash talk through different media outlets. Both spoke out to try to convince fans not to buy the other's album. In an effort to sway people to buy his album, 50 Cent bragged that his album featured rappers Eminem and Dr. Dre, as well as hip-hop singer Justin Timberlake. 50 Cent claimed his album would come out on top. In the end, West won the competition, selling 957,000 copies of *Graduation* in its first six days of sales, compared with *Curtis's* sales of 691,000 copies. An elated West told the ABC television show *Nightline*, however, that he was more concerned about connecting to audiences than making sales. However, West's triumph would soon be overshadowed by a tragic incident.

> "It isn't about the record sales. I'd rather sell, you know, 500,000 records to people who listen to them every single day of their life than a million records to people who didn't listen at all."[4]
>
> —*WEST ON MAKING MUSIC AND RECORD SALES*

DEVASTATING GOOD-BYE

On November 10, 2007, Donda died at age 58 due to complications during plastic surgery. Thirty-year-old West was devastated. As he put it, "It was like losing an arm and a leg and trying to walk through that."[3] On Tuesday, November 20, West and his extended family gathered in Spencer, Oklahoma, outside Donda's childhood home of Oklahoma City, at the True Vine Ministries church. The service was private, though Jay-Z and hip-hop singer Beyoncé attended.

After his mother was laid to rest, rumors flew that West was delusional and close to suicide. He blamed himself for his mother's passing, convinced that if she hadn't quit her job and moved to Los Angeles, where there is so much emphasis on looking perfect, she would have lived. In early 2008, the results from Donda's autopsy came in.

After Donda's failed surgery, then-governor of California Arnold Schwarzenegger passed the Donda West Law, requiring all plastic surgery patients to undergo a complete health check and obtain written consent before any procedure. The new law simply reinforced what was already supposed to be common practice among plastic surgeons. After the law passed, however, many doctors went on record saying it would not have any effect on surgeons who already perform surgeries risky to the patient.

The report stated that Donda had a preexisting problem with her heart that had put her at risk for after-surgery complications. Finding out the reason behind his mother's death did not ease West's pain. While he did cancel a few engagements, a week after his mother's death West performed for an audience of 6,000 in Paris, France, and broke into tears at the opening chords of his ballad "Hey Mama."

||||||||||||||||||||||||||||||||||||||||||||||||||||

PICKING UP THE PIECES

In November, Knievel dropped his lawsuit against Kanye. The two met at Knievel's Clearwater, Florida, condo and settled their differences. Knievel said after spending a little time with West,

West singing his tribute "Hey Mama" during the Grammys
on February 10, 2008

"I thought he was a wonderful guy and quite a
gentleman." He also acknowledged the difficulties
West was facing over his mother's death. "I know
he's had some tough times the past few weeks, and
I hope things work out."[5]

The Grammy Awards honoring 2007 music
were held three months to the day after Donda had
died. West was able to perform without breaking
down and sang a special version of "Hey Mama"
in tribute at the night's awards. He also walked

Many regard West as a perfectionist, especially when it comes to his music. According to Jay-Z, West puts everything into his music and doesn't understand why everyone else doesn't approach things the way he does. Jay-Z has confessed that this sometimes makes him crazy, but also that the result is usually pretty spectacular.

away with four awards: Best Rap Solo Performance ("Stronger"), Best Rap Performance by a Duo or Group ("Southside"), Best Rap Song ("Good Life"), and Best Rap Album (*Graduation*). In his acceptance speech, West honored his mother. He asked that the background music be stopped and spoke to her directly, "I appreciate everything and I know you are really proud of me right now and I know you wouldn't want me to stop and you want me to be the number one artist in the world. And Momma, all I'm gonna do is keep making you proud."[6]

West continued rapping and focused on his music after his mother died. The perfectionist tendencies he had grew stronger as he threw himself into his work. Even before his mother's death, critics noticed West was becoming "smarter and more strategic in his movements."[7] One reporter remarked that if one learned to ignore his ego and had the energy to keep up with him, West made good company. "The biggest misconception is people think I wouldn't be cool to hang around. I think I'm a cool guy to hang around, but then maybe that's just me being arrogant again," he said.[8]

||||||||||||

West performing in 2008

CHAPTER 8
Future Designs

tarting in April 2008, West set out on his worldwide Glow in the Dark Tour. The tour began on April 16 in Seattle, Washington, and ended December 7 in Brisbane, Australia. Fellow artists Rihanna, Lupe Fiasco, N.E.R.D, and Nas were a part of the tour. In an interview three years later, West confessed that the tour allowed him to avoid confronting his sadness over his mother's death. Whatever the motivation, the show got mostly positive reviews. Toward the end of April, rumors swirled that West and fiancée Phifer had split. On April 21, *People* magazine reported the couple had officially called off their engagement.

West kept busy following the breakup. In May, MTV voted him the Number 1 "Hottest MC in the Game."[1] In August, he decided to try his hand at the restaurant business. He and rapper E-40 launched the food company KW Foods and prepared to open several Fatburger chain restaurants in the Chicago area. Two were opened, but as of 2011, one had closed down.

On November 24, West also released a new album, *808s & Heartbreak*. West had recorded the album that fall in California and Hawaii. Seven weeks after its release, *808s & Heartbreak* went platinum. Despite this success, many of West's fans, critics, and peers had mixed feelings about the album. It features West singing 12 emotional and minimalist tracks describing his feelings about losing his mom and girlfriend. Gone were West's wit and wordplay, and there wasn't any objectionable language. West had recorded the entire album in just three weeks that autumn, and most of his beats were laid down with a drum

West's album and performances in 2011 displayed a more emotional, contemplative side to him.

machine that "dated from the dawn of rap, a Roland TR-808," which is how the album got part of its name.[2]

The romantic heartbreak that helped name West's new album didn't last for long. By the beginning of 2009, he had a new girlfriend, model Amber Rose. Rose had a flair for wild fashions, and she and West were often seen attending events in unusual ensembles.

OUTRAGEOUS OUTBURSTS . . . AGAIN

That September, West attended the MTV Video Music Awards. He made a scene at the awards when, for the second time at an MTV awards show, he rushed the stage. But this time, he wasn't even defending his own music. As country singer Taylor Swift was announced as the winner of the Best Female Video and came up to accept her award, West pushed his way on to the stage and grabbed the microphone from a bewildered Swift. He addressed the young star before declaring another nominee should have won. "Yo, Taylor, I'm really happy for you, I'ma let you finish, but Beyoncé had one of the best videos of *all time*. One of the best videos of *all time*."[3] The negative effects from

West takes the microphone from Taylor Swift during her acceptance speech at the MTV Video Music Awards in 2009.

the incident spread worldwide. West was made fun of by bloggers and talk show hosts, and his peers in the music industry shunned him. Even the president of the United States publicly called him out for his behavior. It was the kind of moment that could wreck even the brightest career. The next day, West went on evening talk show host Jay Leno's television show to apologize. West acknowledged his rudeness and then left town. He kept a low profile for months, traveling in Japan and then heading to Italy for a four-month internship with the fashion designer Fendi.

"Whatever you think of the many controversies he has ignited, you must admit that Kanye West is at least some kind of musical genius, ranking among the top five producers and the top five rappers of the past decade. . . . Kanye's power resides in his wild creativity and expressiveness, his mastery of form, and his deep and uncompromising attachment to a self-made aesthetic that he expresses through means that are entirely of the moment: rap music, digital downloads, fashion, Twitter, blogs, live streaming video. He is . . . the Mozart of contemporary American music."[6]

—DAVID SAMUELS, ATLANTIC MAGAZINE

By the beginning of 2010, West was back in the United States and headed to Hawaii to record his next solo album, *My Beautiful Dark Twisted Fantasy*. The album was released on November 22, 2010, and it topped the *Billboard* 200 chart in its first week. It went platinum by January 2011. Although it was still not back to his older sound, reviews for the album were generally glowing. *Spin* magazine rated the album a nine out of ten, praising it as "loud and proud, but also poignant and gripping, always hinting at some looming danger."[7] A *New York Times* music critic wrote that West was truly an innovator, that he "finds different ways to sound phenomenal."[8]

WATCH THE THRONE

West also used social media Web site Twitter to promote his music. In January 2011, he began tweeting about a new project. It appeared West was going to partner with mentor Jay-Z to make an album, *Watch the Throne*. In early January, West and Jay-Z released the single "H.A.M," on a page on social media Web site Facebook after midnight on January 11. By 9 a.m., the song had been played 43,000 times. But then a few months passed without the release of any new material. Rumors flew that the full album might not happen.

A producer told MTV he'd been in Paris to make some beats with the duo and praised the work he said they were doing. "It's not gonna be nothing less of what y'all expect them to do.

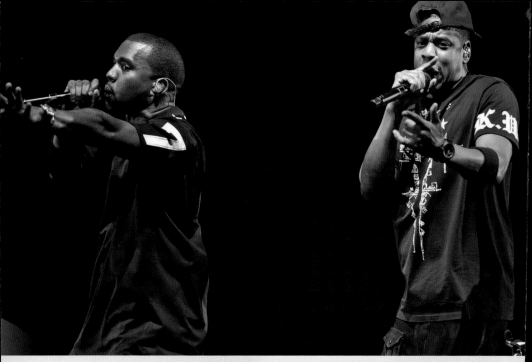

West and Jay-Z performing during a Watch the Throne Tour stop
in Washington DC in November 2011

It's actually on another level," he said.[9] The album
was released on iTunes on August 8, 2011. Within
a week, the album topped Soundscan sales charts,
selling more than 436,000 units. The album
reached Number 1 on iTunes in 23 countries.

The Watch the Throne Tour began in
October 2011 and wrapped in June 2012. Jay-Z
and West extended the tour in the middle, adding
additional shows because the ticket demand
was so high. In January 2012, West unveiled
his plans to create a new design company called

DONDA after his late mother. West tweeted he was currently gathering a team of designers, architects, musicians, tech guys, bankers, and even a nutritionist and doctors for the project. He went on to say the Watch the Throne Tour was an example of the kind of quality production people could expect from his endeavors.

On February 12, West and Jay-Z won the Best Rap Performance Award for the song "Otis" from their collaborated album at the Grammys. West was also nominated for six other Grammy Awards that night, which was more than any other artist that year. West won another three awards that night: Best Rap/Sung Collaboration and Best Rap Song for "All of the Lights," and Best Rap Album for *My Beautiful Dark Twisted Fantasy*. However, West was not present to pick up his many awards, nor was Jay-Z to accept their shared award. There was speculation about why neither West nor Jay-Z attended the 54th Grammy Awards. Some speculated West didn't attend because *My Beautiful Dark Twisted Fantasy* didn't get nominated for Album of the Year.

West's next project was working on his sixth studio album, *Cruel Summer*, which includes contributions from a mix of rappers, hip-hop, and

R&B artists. As a prelude to its release, West wrote, produced, and directed a short experimental film of the same name. It stars rapper Kid Cudi (who is also a G.O.O.D. Music musician) as a car thief who falls for a blind princess. The film was shot in the country of Qatar, on the northeast coast of the Arabian Peninsula, and shown at the Cannes Film Festival on March 23, where it garnered a generally positive response. The album was officially released on September 18, 2012.

The month following the Cannes Film Festival, photographers snapped pictures of West on what looked like a date with reality star Kim Kardashian. As the spring and summer progressed, the rumors that the two were dating proved true. According to the lyrics to "Theraflu," a song by West featuring G.O.O.D. Music artist DJ Khaled that was released in April 2012, West had been interested in Kim for a while, even though she was married. On the song, which a week after release had its title changed to "Way Too Cold," West raps: "I'll admit, I fell in love with Kim/'Round the time she had fell in love with him."[10] The "him" apparently referred to professional basketball player Kris Humphries, whom Kardashian was married to for 72 days

In 2012, West's new relationship with Kim Kardashian was going strong, and his career was in a positive place with a successful tour wrapped and a new album rising on the charts.

before filing for divorce on October 31, 2011. In mid-August, West's relationship with Kardashian appeared still to be going strong as the two vacationed together in Hawaii.

As for West's future career, many critics are confident his success will continue. As West himself puts it: "I will go down as the voice of this generation, of this decade, I will be the loudest voice."[11] Whether that will be true is yet to be seen, but one thing is certain: West will definitely be heard.

||||||||||

TIMELINE

1977

1980

1987

Kanye Omari West is born on June 8.

West moves to Chicago, Illinois, with his mother after his parents' divorce.

West and his mother move to China for one year.

2002

2002

2003

West nearly gets signed as a rapper to Capitol Records, but is instead signed to Roc-A-Fella.

West is in a serious car accident on October 23.

West starts the Kanye West Foundation.

1991

With money he's saved and money he gets for Christmas, West buys his first sampling keyboard.

1998

West drops out of college to pursue a career in rap music.

2001

Jay-Z's album *The Blueprint* is released, for which West has produced some songs.

2003

The lead single "Through the Wire" from West's upcoming debut album, *The College Dropout*, is released on September 30.

2004

West's first album, *The College Dropout*, is released on February 10.

2005

West's second album, *Late Registration*, is released on August 30.

TIMELINE

2005

In September, during a nationally televised fund-raiser for victims of Hurricane Katrina, West makes negative remarks about President George W. Bush.

2006

West gets engaged to girlfriend Alexis Phifer in August.

2006

On November 2, West storms the stage at the MTV European Music Awards when he doesn't win the Best Video Award for "Touch the Sky."

2008

West releases the album *808s & Heartbreak* on November 24.

2009

In September, West interrupts a speech by Taylor Swift at the MTV Video Music Awards.

2010

West releases the album *My Beautiful Dark Twisted Fantasy* on November 22.

2006	2007	2007

In December, Evel Knievel sues West for using his likeness in "Touch the Sky."

West releases his third album, *Graduation*, on September 11.

West's mother, Donda, dies on November 10 from complications related to cosmetic surgery.

2011	2012	2012

West and Jay-Z put out an album together, *Watch the Throne*, on August 8.

In April, it is rumored West and Kim Kardashian are dating. By that summer, it is confirmed.

West releases the album *Cruel Summer* on September 18.

GET THE SCOOP

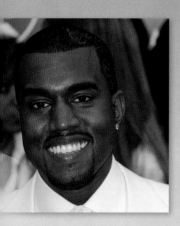

FULL NAME

Kanye Omari West

DATE OF BIRTH

June 8, 1977

PLACE OF BIRTH

Douglasville, Georgia

ALBUMS

The College Dropout (2004), *Late Registration* (2005), *Graduation* (2007), *808s & Heartbreak* (2008), *My Beautiful Dark Twisted Fantasy* (2010), *Watch the Throne* (2011), *Cruel Summer* (2012)

SELECTED TOURS

Glow in the Dark (2008), Watch the Throne (2011)

SELECTED AWARDS

- Won best Rap Album, Best Rap Song, and Best R&B Song at his first Grammy Awards, in 2005
- Won three awards at the Grammy Awards in 2007: Best Rap Song, Best Rap Solo Performance, and Best Rap Album
- Named Best Hip-Hop Artist at the 2006 MTV European Music Awards
- Won Best Rap Album, Best Rap Song, Best Rap Solo Performance, and Best Rap Performance Duo or Group at the Grammy Awards in 2008
- Won Best Rap/Sung Collaboration, Best Rap Song, Best Rap Performance, and Best Rap Album at the Grammy Awards in 2012

PHILANTHROPY

West started the Kanye West Foundation in 2003 with the original mission to help combat high school dropout rates. The charity gave away a college scholarship in 2005. The charity grew to support other causes as well, and in 2005, it provided support for Hurricane Katrina relief efforts.

"I will go down as the voice of this generation, of this decade, I will be the loudest voice."

—KANYE WEST

GLOSSARY

aesthetic—A particular taste for or style of art.

beatsmith—Someone who produces hip-hop or R&B music and creates beats—a beat maker.

Billboard—A music chart system used by the music recording industry to measure record popularity or sales.

chart—A weekly listing of songs or albums in order of popularity or record sales.

collaborate—To work together to create or produce a work, such as a song or album.

debut—A first appearance.

demo—An initial recording meant to demonstrate a musician's talent to a record producer.

genre—A category of art, music, or literature characterized by a particular style, form, or content.

Grammy Award—One of several awards the National Academy of Recording Arts and Sciences presents each year to honor musical achievement.

hip-hop—A style of popular music associated with US urban culture that features rap spoken against a background of electronic music beats.

memoir—A written account of one's experiences.

mentor—A trusted counselor or guide.

platinum—A certification by the Recording Industry Association of America that an album has sold more than 1 million copies. Multiplatinum indicates that the album has sold more than 2 million copies.

producer—Someone who oversees or provides money for a play, television show, movie, or album.

rap—A style of popular music noted for rhythmic speaking of rhymed couplets set to a strong beat.

record label—A brand or trademark related to the marketing of music videos and recordings.

rhythm and blues—A kind of music that—especially in modern times—typically combines hip-hop, soul, and funk.

single—An individual song that is distributed on its own over the radio and other mediums.

speculate—To ponder or reflect on a subject.

studio—A room with electronic recording equipment where music, television, or film is recorded.

track—A portion of a recording containing a single song or a piece of music.

venue—The place where a concert or other event is held.

ADDITIONAL RESOURCES

SELECTED BIBLIOGRAPHY

Ogunnaike, Lola. "Inside Kanye West's World." *Rolling Stone: Music*. Rolling Stone, 23 Nov. 2010. Web. 22 Oct. 2012.

Touré. "Head of the Class." *Rolling Stone* April 29, 2004: 52–54. *Rolling Stone All Access*. Web. 22 Oct. 2012.

West, Donda and Karen Hunter. *Raising Kanye: Life Lessons from the Mother of a Hip-Hop Superstar*. New York: Simon, 2007. *Google Book Search*. Web. 22 Oct. 2012.

FURTHER READINGS

Hoblin, Paul. Jay-Z: *Hip-Hop Mogul*. Minneapolis, MN: ABDO, 2012. Print.

Mattern, Joanne. *Kim Kardashian: Reality TV Star*. Minneapolis, MN: ABDO, 2012. Print.

WEB SITES

To learn more about Kanye West, visit ABDO Publishing Company online at **www.abdopublishing.com**. Web sites about Kanye West are featured on our Book Links page. These links are routinely monitored and updated to provide the most current information available.

PLACES TO VISIT

The Grammy Museum
800 West Olympic Boulevard, Los Angeles, CA 90015
213-765-6800
www.grammymuseum.org
The Grammy Museum features exhibits related to many genres of music.

Museum at the Fashion Institute of Technology
Seventh Avenue at Twenty-Seventh Street, New York City, NY 10001-5992
212-217-4558
fashionmuseum.fitnyc.edu
The Museum at the Fashion Institute of Technology features exhibits and programs dedicated to fashion.

SOURCE NOTES

CHAPTER 1. EXPECTING TO WIN

1. "Kanye West Wins His First Grammy Award." *YouTube*. YouTube, 15 Feb. 2011. Web. 22 Oct. 2012.

2. Ibid.

3. Donda West and Karen Hunter. *Raising Kanye: Life Lessons from the Mother of a Hip-Hop Superstar*. New York: Simon, 2007. *Google Book Search*. Web. 22 Oct. 2012.

4. Karin Nelson. "Intern With Entourage." *New York Times*. New York Times, 3 Dec. 2008. Web. 22 Oct. 2012.

5. "Kanye West and His 'Bazaar' Angel Mural." *New York News & Features*. New York Media, 20 Nov. 2007. Web. 22 Oct. 2012.

CHAPTER 2. BORN CONFIDENT

1. Donda West and Karen Hunter. *Raising Kanye: Life Lessons from the Mother of a Hip-Hop Superstar*. New York: Simon, 2007. *Google Book Search*. Web. 22 Oct. 2012.

2. Ibid.

3. Steve Jones. "Kanye West, Hip-Hop's Writer-in-Residence." *USA Today*. USA Today/Gannett Co., 21 August 2005. Web. 22 Oct. 2012.

4. Touré. "Head of the Class." *Rolling Stone* April 29, 2004: 52–54. *Rolling Stone All Access*. Web. 22 Oct 2012.

5. Donda West and Karen Hunter. *Raising Kanye: Life Lessons from the Mother of a Hip-Hop Superstar*. New York: Simon, 2007. *Google Book Search*. Web. 22 Oct. 2012.

CHAPTER 3. ADVENTURE AND MUSIC

1. Donda West and Karen Hunter. *Raising Kanye: Life Lessons from the Mother of a Hip-Hop Superstar*. New York: Simon, 2007. *Google Book Search*. Web. 22 Oct. 2012.

2. Jake Brown. *Kanye West in the Studio: Beats Down! Money Up!* Phoenix: Colossus Books-Amber, 2006. *Google Book Search*. Web. 22 Oct. 2012.

3. Touré. "Head of the Class." *Rolling Stone* April 29, 2004: 52–54. *Rolling Stone All Access*. Web. 22 Oct 2012.

4. Jake Brown. *Kanye West in the Studio: Beats Down! Money Up!* Phoenix: Colossus Books-Amber, 2006. *Google Book Search*. Web. 22 Oct. 2012.

5. Ibid.

6. Donda West and Karen Hunter. *Raising Kanye: Life Lessons from the Mother of a Hip-Hop Superstar*. New York: Simon, 2007. *Google Book Search*. Web. 22 Oct. 2012.

7. Jake Brown. *Kanye West in the Studio: Beats Down! Money Up!* Phoenix: Colossus Books-Amber, 2006. *Google Book Search*. Web. 22 Oct. 2012.

8. Simon Vozick-Levinson. "Don't Call it a Comeback." *EW.com*.
Entertainment Weekly, 2 Nov. 2007. Web. 22 Oct. 2012.

9. Jake Brown. *Kanye West in the Studio: Beats Down! Money Up!* Phoenix:
Colossus Books-Amber, 2006. *Google Book Search*. Web. 22 Oct. 2012.

CHAPTER 4. MUSICAL AMBITIONS

1. Donda West and Karen Hunter. *Raising Kanye: Life Lessons from the
Mother of a Hip-Hop Superstar*. New York: Simon, 2007. *Google Book Search*.
Web. 22 Oct. 2012.

2. Jake Brown. *Kanye West in the Studio: Beats Down! Money Up!* Phoenix:
Colossus Books-Amber, 2006. *Google Book Search*. Web. 22 Oct. 2012.

3. Corey Moss. "College Dropout Kanye Tells High School Students Not
to Follow in His Footsteps." *MTV*. Viacom International, 5 Dec. 2005. Web.
22 Oct. 2012.

4. Jake Brown. *Kanye West in the Studio: Beats Down! Money Up!* Phoenix:
Colossus Books-Amber, 2006. *Google Book Search*. Web. 22 Oct. 2012.

5. Lola Ogunnaike. "Inside Kanye West's World." *Rolling Stone: Music*.
Rolling Stone, 23 Nov. 2010. Web. 22 Oct. 2012.

CHAPTER 5. CRASH AND SUCCESS

1. Andres Vasquez. "DJ Whoo Kid Shares Untold Story about Kanye
West's Car Accident." *HipHopDX*. Cheri Media Group, 26 Jan. 2012. Web.
22 Oct. 2012.

2. Shaheem Reid. "Kanye West Raps through His Broken Jaw, Lays Beats
for Scarface, Ludacris." *MTV*. Viacom International, 10 Dec. 2002. Web.
22 Oct. 2012.

3. Dave Heaton. "Kanye West: The College Dropout." *PopMatters*.
PopMatters.com, 5 Mar. 2004. Web. 22 Oct. 2012.

4. Ibid.

5. Donda West and Karen Hunter. *Raising Kanye: Life Lessons from
the Mother of a Hip-Hop Superstar*. New York: Simon, 2007. *Amazon*. Web.
22 Oct. 2012.

6. "Take it From Me: Kanye West." *MH Celebrity Fitness*. Rodale, n.d.
Web. 22 Oct. 2012.

7. Tanya M. Fowlow. "GLC: Space Age Pimpin'." *HipHopDX*. Cheri
Media Group, 12 July 2010. Web. 22 Oct. 2012.

8. Chris Willman. "One Sorry Nom." *EW.com*. Entertainment Weekly,
13 Dec. 2012. Web. 22 Oct. 2012.

9. "All Eyes on Kanye West." *MTV*. MTV Networks, n.d. Web.
22 Oct. 2012.

10. Simon Vozick-Levinson. "Jay-Z's Brotherly Love." *EW.com*.
Entertainment Weekly, 20 Sept. 2007. Web. 22 Oct. 2012.

11. "All Eyes on Kanye West." *MTV*. MTV Networks, n.d. Web. 22 Oct. 2012.

CHAPTER 6. CHANGING HIP-HOP

1. Josh Tyrangiel/Prague. "Why You Can't Ignore Kanye." *TIME*. Time, 21 Aug. 2005. Web. 23 Oct. 2012.

2. "'Hey Mama' Lyrics." *MetroLyrics*. MetroLyrics.com, n.d. Web. 23 Oct. 2012.

3. Donda West and Karen Hunter. *Raising Kanye: Life Lessons from the Mother of a Hip-Hop Superstar*. New York: Simon, 2007. *Google Book Search*. Web. 22 Oct. 2012.

4. Rob Sheffield. "Kanye West: *Late Registration*, Def Jam." *Rolling Stone: Reviews*. Rolling Stone, 25 Aug. 2005. Web. 23 Oct. 2012.

5. Lisa de Moraes. "Kanye West's Torrent of Criticism, Live on NBC." *Washington Post*. Washington Post, 3 Sept. 2005. Web. 23 Oct. 2012.

6. Ibid.

7. Marla Lehner. "Kanye West Defends Anti-Bush Comments." *People*. Time, 9 Sept. 2005. Web. 23 Oct. 2012.

8. Ibid.

9. Ibid.

CHAPTER 7. LOVE AND LOSS

1. Kristin Braswell. "Kanye West's History of Outbursts." *ABC News*. ABC News, 14 Sept. 2009. Web. 23 Oct. 2012.

2. Associated Press. "Evil [sic] Knievel Sues Kanye West Over Video." *Today: Music*. NBCNews.com, 12 Dec. 2006. Web. 23 Oct. 2012.

3. Andres Vasquez. "Kanye West Speaks Candidly about Mother, Religion, Rap." *HipHopDX*. Cheri Media Group, 2 Dec. 2008. Web. 23 Oct. 2012.

4. Eric Johnson. "Kanye West: Hip-Hop's 'Creative Genius.'" *ABC Nightline*. ABC News Internet Ventures, 23 Sept. 2007. Web. 23 Oct. 2012.

5. Associated Press. "Evel Knievel, Kanye West Settle Lawsuit." *USA Today*. USA Today/Gannett Co., 27 Nov. 2007. Web. 23 Oct. 2012.

6. "Grammy Gabfest: Kanye West." *CBSNews*. CBS Interactive, n.d. Web. 23 Oct. 2012.

7. Jon Caramanica. "The Education of Kanye West." *New York Times*. New York Times, 26 Aug. 2007. Web. 23 Oct. 2012.

8. Luke Bainbridge. "It's Kanye's World." *The Guardian/The Observer*. Guardian News and Media, 11 Aug. 2007. Web. 23 Oct. 2012.

CHAPTER 8. FUTURE DESIGNS

1. Shaheem Reid. "Hottest MCs In The Game': At Last, We Agree With Kanye West—He Is #1." *MTV*. Viacom International, 16 May 2008. Web. 23 Oct. 2012.

2. Ivan Solotaroff. "The Unraveling of Kanye West." *Details*. Condé Nast, n.d. Web. 23 Oct. 2012.

3. David Samuels. "American Mozart." *Atlantic*. Atlantic Monthly Group, May 2012. Web. 23 Oct. 2012.

4. Lola Ogunnaike. "Inside Kanye West's World." *Rolling Stone: Music*. Rolling Stone, 23 Nov. 2010. Web. 22 Oct. 2012.

5. Donda West and Karen Hunter. *Raising Kanye: Life Lessons from the Mother of a Hip-Hop Superstar*. New York: Simon, 2007. *Amazon*. Web. 22 Oct. 2012.

6. David Samuels. "American Mozart." *Atlantic*. Atlantic Monthly Group, May 2012. Web. 23 Oct. 2012.

7. Chris Martins. "Kanye West, 'My Beautiful Dark Twisted Fantasy.'" *Spin*. Spin, 22 Nov. 2010. Web. 23 Oct. 2012.

8. Jon Caramanica. "Kanye West, Still Unfiltered, on Eve of Fifth Album." *New York Times*. New York Times, 17 Nov. 2010. Web. 23 Oct. 2012.

9. Rob Markman. "Kanye West, Jay-Z Tap Bangladesh for Watch the Throne." *MTV*. Viacom International, 2 May 2011. Web. 23 Oct. 2012.

10. Rebecca Macatee. "Aw! Kanye West Sings to Girlfriend Kim Kardashian at Atlantic City Concert." *E!* E! Entertainment Television/NBCUniversal, 9 July 2012. Web. 23 Oct. 2012.

11. Louise Dixon. "Kanye West: I'm The 'Voice of this Generation.'" *USA Today*. USA Today/Gannett Co., 13 Nov. 2008. Web. 23 Oct. 2012.

INDEX

ABOUT THE AUTHOR

Douglas Lynne is a freelance writer. He spent many years working in the media, first in newspapers and later for online organizations, covering everything from breaking news to politics to entertainment to sports. He lives in Minneapolis, Minnesota.

PHOTO CREDITS